# The Lion's Whiskers

"The Lion's Share"

# The Lion's Whiskers
## and Other Ethiopian Tales

BY BRENT ASHABRANNER
AND RUSSELL DAVIS

REVISED EDITION BY
BRENT ASHABRANNER

ILLUSTRATIONS BY HELEN SIEGL

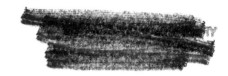

Linnet Books
1997

Library of Congress Cataloging-in-Publication Data
The lion's whiskers and other Ethiopian tales / [edited] by Brent
Ashabranner and Russell Davis ; illustrations by Helen Siegl.—
Rev. ed. / by Brent K. Ashabranner.
p.   cm.
Rev. ed. of: The lion's whiskers : tales of high Africa / by
Russell Davis and Brent K. Ashabranner.
Summary: A collection of folktales from the nine main tribes of
Ethiopia, along with two stories from Ethiopia's religious
traditions.
ISBN 0-208-02429-8 (lib. bdg. : alk. paper)
1. Tales—Ethiopia. [1. Folklore—Ethiopia.]  I. Ashabranner,
Brent, 1921–  , II. Davis, Russell G.  III. Siegl, Helen, ill.
IV. Lion's whiskers.
PZ8.1.L664   1997
398.2'0963—dc21       97-3981
CIP     AC

The paper in this publication meets the
minimum requirements of
American National Standard for Information Sciences—
Permanence of Paper for Printed Library Materials, ANSI Z39.48-1984. ⊗

Designed by Abigail Johnston
Printed in the United States of America

*This edition of* The Lion's Whiskers *is dedicated to the memory of Russell Davis, my good friend, writing partner, and colleague in international educational assistance.*
BRENT ASHABRANNER

# Contents

# Acknowledgments

I wish to thank Mr. Ayalew Yiman, Counselor, Embassy of Ethiopia, Washington, D.C., for his patient help in refreshing my memory of certain Ethiopian words and customs. If I have made mistakes in the pages ahead, they are my own, not his.

I also wish to thank my daughter Jennifer Ashabranner for her research assistance on parts of this revised edition of *The Lion's Whiskers*. Jennifer experienced Ethiopia when she was very young, between the ages of three and five; but she still has good memories of some of her friends, of our family's long vacation road trip from Addis Ababa to the Red Sea port of Massawa in Eritrea, and especially of her pet monkey Chip.

# Editor's Note
# The Story Behind the Stories

**T**his is a book of stories that Russell Davis and I collected when we worked in the African country of Ethiopia for two years during the 1950s. The original edition of *The Lion's Whiskers*, published in 1959, went through seven printings and stayed in print for a number of years. During those years we heard from many readers about the stories. For this new edition I have selected the ones that have been liked best by teachers, folklorists, and—most important—by children. Most of the stories are folktales, two are from Ethiopia's rich religious traditions, and one or two relate our personal experiences.

A land of towering mountains and what the eighteenth-century traveler James Bruce called "valleys of dreadful depth," Ethiopia is in northeastern Africa; but it does not fit neatly, either culturally or geographically, as a part of North Africa (Egypt, Libya, Morocco, Algeria) or with such East African countries as Kenya and Tanzania. Some geographers simply say that Ethiopia is in the "horn" of Africa.

Historians also have had their problems with Ethiopia. According to Ethiopian tradition, the kingdom of Ethiopia was founded about the ninth century B.C. by Emperor Menelik I. Again according to tradition, Menelik was the son of King Solomon and the Queen of Sheba. The first recorded kingdom in the area that is now Ethiopia, however, was Aksum. Aksum probably was founded by traders from Arabia in the first century A.D. and was converted to Christianity in the fourth century. Ethiopia has remained a Christian country since that time, although a considerable part of the population today is Muslim.

Because of its isolation and rugged terrain, Ethiopia slipped from the pages of European history during the Middle Ages; one later historian wrote that it "wrapped itself in a cloak and slept for a thousand years." During the Crusades to recapture the Holy Land from the Arabs, Europeans began to hear stories of a great African kingdom ruled by a Christian emperor called Prester John. English and French kings sent emissaries looking for Prester John, hoping he would help them in the fight for the Holy Land. They did not find Prester John, but in time Ethiopia was "rediscovered."

Except for a brief period of brutal Italian occupation beginning in 1936, Ethiopia has always been an independent country. With British help the Italian yoke was thrown off in 1941, and the exiled emperor Haile Selassie returned to Addis Ababa, the capital, to resume his rulership of the poor but proud country.

In his inaugural address after his election in 1948, U.S. President Harry Truman proposed a "bold new program" of technical assistance to the poor countries of Africa, Asia, and Latin America, and, after much deliberation, Congress approved the president's proposal. Ethiopia was one of the first countries to request help, and Russ Davis and I were in the vanguard of Americans who wanted to be a part of the new program to assist developing countries with their problems of agriculture, health, and education.

Of course, we were not sent to Ethiopia to collect folktales, but the stories became an important part of our work. Our job was to help the Ethiopian Ministry of Education prepare books for their schools. Working with eager young Ethiopians in the Ministry, we helped to put out a series of arithmetic books, primers, and readers for the elementary and middle schools of Ethiopia. These were among the first such books that had ever been written for Ethiopian school children in Amharic, the country's official language.

Gathering materials for the books and testing what we were preparing took us to all parts of the country, and we came to know every major Ethiopian ethnic group: the Amhara, Oromo (Galla), Tigray, Somali, Beta Israel (Falasha), and others. Each group has its own cultural individuality, including its own language. We learned Amharic, which is widely spoken throughout the country. Russ became fluent; I struggled but never quit learning.

We traveled by Land Rover, always with two or three of our Ethiopian colleagues. We slept under the stars, sometimes on the floor of a schoolhouse, occasionally in a hotel bed. We talked to headmasters, teachers, and students in every town we passed through; the message from teachers was always the same: Send us books to teach with. We talked to farmers, village leaders, and old men and women who told us stories they had heard from their parents and grandparents. Many of those stories, real Ethiopian stories, went into the schoolbooks we were preparing.

A year or so after we left Ethiopia, Russ and I wrote an article for *The Horn Book Magazine* about our first trip through the country. The title of the article was "Harvesting Folk Tales," and here is the way it began:

Haik is a lovely lake high in the mountains of central Ethiopia. *Haik* is actually the Amharic word for lake, but so important is this body of water to the people living around it that it has no other name. It is simply *Haik,* the lake. It gives the lake dwellers abundant fish; it gives them water; it gives them reeds for mats and for their curious little boats. On a small island at its center, it shelters the ancient and revered monastery of Saint Stephen.

We were on our way to Aksum, holy city of Ethiopia, and had stopped to make night camp at the edge of *Haik.* As we unloaded our Land Rover, an old monk from Saint Stephen's wandered by and stopped to watch us. We talked to him, and he told us that he was a bird watcher in a monastery cornfield nearby. All day long he sat on a little elevated platform in the center of the field and threw rocks to frighten away the marauding birds.

"It is a job for children or very old men," he said. "The child will do the job because he becomes interested in it. The old man will do the job because he has patience."

"But it is an important job," we said.

"Oh, yes," he agreed. "It is important. Without the watcher, birds would grow fat and men would starve. God is good to give old men such important work."

"Have you been many years at the monastery?" we asked him.

"Since I was a boy of eight," the old monk replied.

Here seemed to be just the man we were looking for: one old enough in the area to know its oral traditions, clear-minded enough to remember details, possessed of a certain facility with words, and holding a clear set of beliefs and values. Such a combination often returns rich dividends for the folklorist.

Our man was as good as he promised to be. We drew him out slowly, and as shadows lengthened beside our Land Rover, he told us story after story that he had heard since his boyhood. Once he was warmed up, he felt no shyness about talking into the microphone of our battery-run tape recorder. In fact, after he heard his own voice on our playback, he seemed to enjoy himself immensely.

Inevitably, many of his stories dealt with the lake that was so important to the life of the region. He told us of the wicked people who had once made human sacrifices to a huge water serpent which they believed to be the spirit of the lake. He told us of a great holy man who came into the land and was outraged at the wickedness of the lake people. The holy man set the waters of the lake afire to show the people the power of the true God; from that day they were all Christians, and the monastery of Saint Stephen was founded. The old monk told us how the clever monkey had tricked all the other animals into thinking that the lake water was poison so that he could have it all to himself.

Later, as we sat around our campfire, the old bird watcher's tales lingered and sharpened our awareness of the sights and sounds around us: the night cries of unseen animals; the moonlight floating like a golden film on the lake; the dark, crouching bulk of the encircling mountains.

By the time we returned to our homes in Addis Ababa, we knew infinitely more about Ethiopia than we had before the trip began.

# 1
# The Hyena Man

In the ancient town of Harar in the high African country of Ethiopia there lives an old Somali man named Mohammed Moshin. His home is a one-room mud *tukal* near the *Budaber* (the Gate of the Evil-eyed People), but his fame is great in the land. Indeed, you will be told by all of the wise people from Dire Dawa to the Ogaden that he is a wizard. For Mohammed can do a great thing. He can charm the wildest and most untamable of all African animals, the cowardly hyena.

We first heard of Mohammed as we drove our Land Rover from Addis Ababa across the Great Rift Valley to Harar, and we went to see him the same night we reached that town. We came to his grass-roofed house just after dark and found him sitting silently before a small fire near his doorway.

We introduced ourselves and said, "We have heard that you have a great power over the wild hyena."

The old man did not seem surprised by our unannounced visit. He pulled his white *shamma* closer about his shoulders. "It is true," he said. "Come inside."

The room was small, but the feebly flickering kerosene lantern hanging from a eucalyptus pole only partially lighted it.

"Sit in the shadows," Mohammed said, "and do not speak."

From a corner he took a pile of bloody sheep bones and sat down cross-legged in the middle of the dirt floor. We had expected him to chant or beat a drum or use some magic device, but instead he began to talk just as if he were speaking to people outside.

"Abdullah," he called, "are you out there? Maymoonah, I have a nice bone for you. Zachariah, are you hungry tonight?"

He called other names, and in less than a minute we began to hear the soft padding of feet and low deep-throated growls from the darkness outside. And then we saw them: more than a dozen huge, shaggy-coated hyenas moving restlessly back and forth in front of the *tukal* door. Occasionally, one would stop and peer inside and then jump back into the darkness in great fright.

"Maymoonah," the old man called, "I know you are there. Come in or I will give this bone to another."

That seemed to do the trick. One of the hyenas, a

big buff-colored beast, halted in the doorway, and, after hesitating for almost a minute, put her head into the hut. Mohammed held a meaty bone out to her and coaxed her softly. The hyena's eyes blazed toward the shadows where we sat, and she backed up a step. But then her hunger seemed to conquer her fear; she slunk into the room with the ugly, broken-back gait that all hyenas have and snatched the bone from the wizard's hand. Instantly she bolted through the door and out into the safety of the darkness. We could hear her crunching the bone in her powerful jaws, and the growls of the other hyenas grew louder.

Maymoonah's bravery seemed to give courage to the rest of the pack, for the giant called Abdullah came in at once when Mohammed shouted his name. After that they came in eagerly, and sometimes as many as three hyenas were in the room at the same time. But always, as soon as they had their bone, they would scramble frantically through the door.

When the pile of sheep bones was finished, Mohammed called, "It is enough. Be gone." And instantly the sounds of growling and restlessly padding feet were gone from the yard outside the little hut. The silence was complete.

It was then that the old wizard turned to us for the first time. "Tonight was not good," he said. "My friends

were afraid because strangers were present. It is my cus-
tom to make them sit down in front of me and eat.''

"We are amazed at what we have seen," we said.
"Can you tell us how you do this thing?"

"I learned it from my father," Mohammed replied,
"who learned it from his father before him."

"Is it magic?" we asked him.

"A kind of magic," the old man said.

"Can you do the same with any animal?"

"Of course."

"Even with a lion?" we asked.

"Yes," Mohammed said, "and even with a child,
which is sometimes hardest of all."

"We do not understand," we told him.

The old wizard smiled. "Have you heard the story
of the woman Bizunesh who could not win the love of
her stepchild Segab?" he asked.

"No," we said, "but we would like very much to
hear it."

And that night, in a smoky one-room *tukal* in the
Ethiopian town of Harar, Mohammed Moshin, the
hyena man, told us the story of the lion's whiskers.

# 2
# The Lion's Whiskers

**B**izunesh, a woman of the Ethiopian highlands, married Gudina, a man of the lowlands. Gudina's first wife had died of a fever, and he had an eight-year-old son whose name was Segab. When Bizunesh went to the house of Gudina, she quickly saw that Segab was a very sad boy because he missed his mother so much.

In only a short time Bizunesh grew to love Segab as if he were her own son, and she tried to be a good mother. She mended all of Segab's clothes and bought him new shoes. She asked him what foods he liked best, and she always saved the choicest pieces of meat from the *wat* for Segab. But Segab did not thank her. He would not even look at her or talk to her.

Bizunesh and Segab were often alone together because Gudina was a merchant who traveled with mule caravans to distant places. Bizunesh worried that Segab would be lonely and tried especially hard to please him when his father was away. "I have always wanted a son," Bizunesh told Segab. "Now God has given me one. I love you very much." Often she tried to kiss him.

But always Segab would turn away from her, and once he shouted, "You are not my mother. I do not love you."

One day Segab ran away from the house and hid in the town market until his father came and found him. When Segab returned home, Bizunesh tried to take him in her arms, but he pulled away from her. He would not touch the bowl of delicious soup she had saved for him. Bizunesh cried all that night.

In the morning Bizunesh went to the hut of a famous wise man. She told the wise man about her new stepson who refused to love her, no matter how hard she tried to please him.

"You must make me a magic love powder," Bizunesh told the old man. "I will put it in Segab's food, and then he will love me."

The wise man was silent for several minutes. "I can do what you ask," he said at last. "But to make such a powder, I must have three whiskers from the ferocious lion who lives in the black-rock desert across the river. Bring the whiskers to me, and I will make the powder for you."

Bizunesh could hardly believe her ears. "How can I get the lion's whiskers?" she asked. "He will surely kill me."

"I cannot tell you how to get the whiskers," the wise man said to Bizunesh. "That is for you to decide. But I must have them before I can make the love powder."

Bizunesh walked sadly from the wise man's hut. She did not sleep a wink that night, but in the morning her mind was made up. Nothing was as important to her as winning Segab's love. She had to try to get three whiskers from the lion even if he ate her. Only then would the wise man make the magic love powder for her.

That very day Bizunesh carried a large piece of raw meat to the black-rock desert. At last she saw the lion standing on a large rock, watching her from a great distance. When the lion jumped from the rock and loped toward her, Bizunesh was terrified. She threw the meat on the ground and ran. Only when she reached the river did she stop and look back. She saw the lion standing over the meat she had dropped. She heard him roar before he began to eat.

Two days later Bizunesh went again to the black-rock desert with a big piece of meat. She saw the lion watching her from the same rock. This time she walked closer to him before the lion jumped down and started toward her. Bizunesh stood still for a moment and watched the lion approach. Then her fear overcame her, and she threw the meat down and ran. When she looked back, she saw the lion eating.

On the following day Bizunesh walked even closer to the lion. This time she placed the meat on the ground and walked slowly away. Before she had gone far she stopped and watched as the lion came and ate the meat.

Day after day Bizunesh came closer. Finally, she left the meat only a hundred feet from the lion. The great beast growled, but Bizunesh did not think it sounded like an angry growl. She moved only a few steps away before she stopped and watched the lion eat. The next day Bizunesh left the meat fifty feet from the lion and stayed while he came and ate.

Then a few days later Bizunesh walked right up to the lion and handed him the meat. Her heart pounded with fear, but her love for Segab was so great that she did not run.

She watched the lion's great jaws fly open! Crash shut! She heard the sound of his teeth tearing through the meat. After a moment she reached out with a very sharp knife and cut three whiskers from the lion's muzzle. The lion was so busy eating that he did not even notice.

Bizunesh ran all the way to the wise man's hut. She

was out of breath, but she was still able to shout, "I have the lion's whiskers!" She waved them in front of the old wise man. "Now make me the love powder, and Segab will surely love me."

The wise man took the lion's whiskers. He looked at them and then handed them back to Bizunesh. "You do not need a love powder," he told her. "You learned how to approach the lion—slowly. Do the same with Segab, and he will learn to love you."

When Mohammed had finished his story, we were smiling. "Now we understand," we said. "Bizunesh learned that important things must sometimes be done a little bit at a time and that one must be patient for results."

"Yes," said Mohammed, "and that is the secret of my magic with the hyenas."

"You are a wise man, Mohammed," we said.

Again Mohammed pulled his *shamma* close about him, for the night was growing chill. "I am a very old man," he replied. "I have never been to school, but I have sat around many village fires and listened when things were talked about and stories were told."

"We have heard many stories in Ethiopia," we said, "and have liked them."

"A good storyteller knows that you must like his stories," Mohammed said, "or you will not come again

to listen. He also knows that you must sometimes learn something from his stories or you will soon know that they are not worth listening to.''

''Where do stories like the one about Bizunesh and Segab come from?'' we asked.

The old man shrugged his shoulders. ''Who knows?'' he said. ''They have been told in my country for so long that no one knows who told them first.''

Mohammed grew silent, and we knew that he was tired. We said good night to him and left his *tukal*. As we drove away in our Land Rover, the headlight beams stabbed into the darkness. From many a bush they caught the bright yellow spots of large hyena eyes.

Later that night when Russ and I talked about our visit with Mohammed, we agreed that the old hyena man had given us a perfect definition of a folktale: a story that has been told for so long that no one knows who told it first, a story you like to listen to, a story that sometimes makes you just a little wiser than you were before you heard it.

# 3
# The King's Black Curtain

We heard many folktales about kings during our travels. That is not surprising because for thousands of years Ethiopia was ruled by kings. While we were in the country, Emperor Haile Selassie was on the throne, and he was considered one of Ethiopia's greatest rulers. Among his many titles were "King of Kings" and "Conquering Lion of Judah." From the very first emperor, Menelik I, all rulers of Ethiopia have been of the Amhara ethnic group. Not unexpectedly, most king stories were told to us by Amhara storytellers. The following story makes clear that a good king must be fair and wise.

Many years ago Ethiopian kings were considered to be almost gods. For that reason it was thought to be improper for anyone, even a nobleman, to see a king eat. In the king's banquet hall there was a long table

13

for the noblemen and a smaller table for the king.
Whenever the king came to his table, a black curtain
was always put up in front of him so that none of the
noblemen could watch him eat. The king could talk to
his guests and they could talk to him, but he could not
be seen until after the meal was over.

On one particular feast day the nobles of the court
were gathered at the palace arguing about who would
be seated nearest the king's table at the dinner that
night. It was considered a great honor to be seated near
the king, for then it was possible to talk to him throughout the meal, even with the curtain drawn across his
table. This arguing among the noblemen went on every
time there was to be a feast. It was pointless arguing,
however, because the king always made up his own
mind who would be seated nearest to him.

On this special day a very well-known teacher came
to the king's court. This teacher was famous throughout the land for his wisdom and for the truth of his
teachings. Nevertheless, he was a humble man who had
never before been to the king's city.

The noblemen were surprised to see a mere
teacher at the court, and one of them said to him
laughingly, "Have you come to join the feast?"

The other nobles laughed at the idea of a teacher,
however wise, attending the king's dinner. The teacher
himself smiled at the question. "No," he said, "I have

come only to pay my respects to the king and to bow before him, for I believe that he is a great and good king."

Some of the noblemen thought that the king would not even take time to see the teacher; but when the king heard that the wise old man was at the palace, he sent for him at once. The noblemen then went back to their arguing and forgot about the teacher.

When they gathered for the feast that night, the nobles were greatly surprised to see that the king had asked the teacher to attend the dinner. But when the nobles sat down at their long table, their surprise turned to shock and anger, for the teacher did not sit down with them. Instead, the king took the old teacher by the arm and led him behind the black curtain to eat at the king's own private table!

One of the bolder noblemen rose and called out in a complaining voice, "O King, never have you given such honor to even the greatest of your nobles. Why do you give this honor to a poor teacher?"

The king came from behind the curtain, and all of the nobles rose from their chairs. "Who made you a *ras*?" the king asked the man who had complained.

"You did, sire," the man replied. "You gave me that title."

The king pointed to another nobleman. "Who made you a *grazmatch*?" he asked.

"You did, sire," the man answered.

The king pointed to still another. "Who made you a *kenyazmatch?*" he asked.

"You did, sire," the man said.

The king looked at every nobleman in turn and asked, "Who made the teacher behind that curtain the wise man that he is?"

The noblemen looked at each other and none could answer the question.

Then the king turned to them, "I can create noblemen. I can take any poor man from the street and give him a title and make him rich and powerful. But only God can create such a wise man as the teacher who eats with me tonight. For this reason his honor is greater than yours."

The king went back behind his black curtain where the teacher awaited him. The nobles sat down again and fell silently to eating, ashamed of the jealousy that had angered them.

# 4
# The Snake in the Bottle

**H**ere is another Amhara story, actually a story within a story, that also emphasizes the wisdom and power of a king.

A king out of the west traveled north and south and east and fought great battles and took much treasure. Since the king was always at war, he built a treasure room and hired a man to guard it.

Now the guard of the treasure room was very careful to keep others from stealing the riches of the king. But the guard himself began to steal the king's treasure. For many years the guard took the treasure, little by little, to a storehouse of his own. The guard emptied the king's chests of gold and silver and jewels and filled them with stones and pebbles.

When the king was old and crippled from his wounds, he returned to his palace to enjoy his treasure.

The guard came before the king and said, "Now Your Majesty has returned. There is a lion in the house once more and so no need for an old guard such as I. Who can guard the treasure better than you, my king?"

"You have spoken the truth," the king said. "And you have served me well for many years. Take this sack of gold and go on your way. Live your remaining days in peace and plenty."

After the guard had gone, the king discovered that his chests were filled with stones and pebbles. The king sent horsemen out to bring the dishonest guard back. The guard tried to escape into another country, but his mules were heavily laden with gold and other treasure and had to go slowly. The horsemen found the guard still within the kingdom and stopped him.

"His Majesty bids you return to his palace," the leader of the horsemen said. "He wishes to speak to you."

"Why does he wish to speak to me?" the guard asked.

"He has not given any reason," the troop commander said. "But you must return."

When the guard was brought back to the palace, the king told him to sit down in the throne room. "I would like to tell you a very short story," the king said. "Once a snake crawled into a farmhouse and found an open bottle of milk. The snake crawled in through the narrow neck of the bottle and began to drink all of the milk. The snake drank and drank until he was too fat to crawl back through the neck of the bottle.''

The king stopped speaking and smiled.

''Is that the end of the story?'' the guard asked. ''It is good to see Your Majesty again; but I have a long journey, and I should be off.''

''That is not quite the end of the story,'' the king said. ''What must the snake do to get out of the bottle?''

''The snake must spit out the milk,'' the guard answered.

''True,'' the king said. ''Must he spit out all of it?''

''I think he will have to spit out all of it to get out,'' the guard said.

''You are right,'' the king said. ''All of it.''

The guard looked up and saw soldiers with spears moving slowly toward him from every door of the throne room.

We can imagine that the guard ''spit out'' all of the stolen treasure, just as the king suggested in his story about the snake trapped in the bottle. But we don't know what happened to the thieving guard after that. Like many good stories, ''The Snake in the Bottle'' leaves us with something to think about.

# 5
# Digit the Midget

Stories about tiny, thumb-sized children appear in the folk traditions and literature of many countries. Tom Thumb, Thumbelina, and Stuart Little are perhaps most familiar to Americans. Amhara children (and grown-ups) enjoy the adventures of a clever, tiny Ethiopian boy named Sinzero. The name "Sinzero" comes from the Amharic word *sinzer,* the measure of the distance from the tip of the thumb to the tip of the longest finger. We have translated Sinzero as "Digit."

Actually, there are two thumblings in Ethiopian folklore. The other is Aure Tat, from the word for thumb. Both Aure Tat and Digit appear in dozens of stories. In the one we have chosen, Digit is a trickster, as he is in most stories about him. The trickster, whether animal or human, is a favorite folk character in all countries and cultures.

Not all folktales have a special meaning or teach

some truth about life. Many, like all of the stories about Digit, are told just for fun.

A woman of Munz had seven large, strong, stupid sons. These sons went about the house breaking chairs with their weight, emptying the *injera* basket and the *wat* pot with their great appetites, and filling the house with the terrifying rumble of their snoring. Although they were very strong, they never worked when they could avoid it. They ate, slept, snored, and got in the way of their poor, hard-working mother.

One day the poor woman of Munz could stand her house and her family no longer. She ran away toward the monastery of Saint Stephen on an island in the lake Haik. The woman was not allowed to go out to the island and the monastery. No woman had been allowed there since the monastery had been built hundreds of years before. The woman from Munz knelt down on the lake shore, cast her eyes toward the holy monastery on the island, and cried in a loud voice:

"O, God and all your angels and saints, hear my prayer! I have been sent seven of the biggest, clumsiest, hungriest, and laziest sons in Ethiopia. Soon I am to have another child. I would like a daughter. But if you do not wish to send me a daughter, please send me a small son."

Now God, who hears all prayers but answers only

some, did not send a daughter, but he did send a small son—a very small son. When Digit was born he was only the length of a man's thumb. The woman of Munz was delighted with her little child. He was the first baby she had ever been able to carry in her arms. For all the other babies, the mother had had to hire a mule to bring them home.

When the days passed and Digit did not grow larger, the mother was even more pleased. And it was clear to her that Digit was a very clever baby and, later, a clever little boy. Digit had to be clever to dodge the feet of his huge, clumsy brothers. Often Digit's mother barely saved him from being crushed by one of his brother's elbows. Another time, when the door was left open, Digit was blown out into the yard by the breeze of his brothers' snoring. Digit's mother always held him close to her, safe from mice and chickens.

As the years passed, the seven huge brothers came to hate Digit. Even when they had been babies and sick, their mother had never taken them on her lap. Their mother had never kissed them on the tops of their heads. She had never even seen the tops of their heads. She had never hugged them because her arms would not fit around them. And once when the oldest brother hugged his mother, he broke three of her ribs. It was clear that Digit was her favorite. She took the choicest meat from the *wat* for Digit, and the brothers had to crack the bones and pick out the marrow for him.

The brothers plotted and schemed to get rid of Digit. Once they persuaded him to steal the prize bull of their most terrible neighbor, who was a *cherak,* a man-eating monster. The brothers thought that the *cherak* would catch and eat Digit. But Digit climbed into the bull's ear. When Digit wished the bull to turn right, he buzzed like a horsefly in the bull's left ear. The bull would turn right to escape the fly. To make a left turn, Digit walked all the way across the bull's neck and buzzed in the right ear. Digit took the bull right out from under the *cherak*'s nose and guided it to the forest where the brothers waited.

The brothers were sorry that Digit had escaped, but they were happy to get the bull. They made a big fire and killed and dressed the bull. They then took all the choice meat for themselves and left Digit none.

Digit said, "Brothers, you are big and you need the meat. All I wish for is the bladder."

Digit's brothers did not want the bladder and threw it to him. Digit then puffed air into the bladder and made a drum. He began to beat on the drum with a stick and shouted, "We stole your prize bull, *Cherak.* Come and get us if you dare. My big brothers are not afraid of your evil spells."

The brothers were terrified. They were so frightened that they threw the meat on the ground and ran away into the forest. Digit went back to the *cherak*'s house, stole a mule, and loaded the meat onto it. Then he brought the meat home and gave it to his mother. He also gave her the mule. The mother made a stew of the hoofs and tail of the bull for her big lazy sons.

Things grew worse. Digit's brothers complained, "Mama never hugs and kisses us. She never calls us her little stalks of sugar like she does Digit. With the little fiend gone, Mama would love us again."

Finally things became so bad that Digit had to move out of the house to his own little house. The mother was so angry that she made her seven big sons leave the home and get married.

One night Digit's brothers burned down his house. But Digit was not killed. He slipped through a hole in the floor into a rabbit's tunnel. Digit walked through the tunnel to safety.

The next morning Digit decided to leave Munz to escape his brothers. He loaded the ashes of his house into sacks and had the sacks loaded onto mules. On the road the first night Digit stopped at the house of a rich man. In the morning when he looked into his sacks, he began to scream, "Robbery! Thief! Some thief took my flour and filled the sacks with ashes!"

Digit screamed and screamed, and the rich man

felt very sorry for the poor little boy. He did not want his neighbors to think that he would steal flour from such a tiny person, so he gave Digit seven new sacks of his own flour. Digit decided to return to his mother's home and give the flour to her.

Digit then told his large, stupid brothers how he had tricked the rich man. "A very clever trick," they all agreed. They went back to their own houses, burned them down, and loaded the ashes into sacks and the sacks onto mules.

The first brother went to the home of the rich man and spent the night. The next morning he opened his sacks of ashes and began to scream that he had been robbed—just as Digit had done. But the rich man ordered him out of the house. When the second brother came along the next day and tried the same trick, the rich man had his servants throw him into the road. When the third brother arrived, the rich man ordered his servants to beat him with sticks.

When the fourth brother came to the house, the rich man asked, "What do you have in those sacks?"

"Flour," the brother said.

"That is good," the rich man said. "We are short of flour. We will make your bread tonight with your flour."

That night the fourth brother had to eat bread made of ashes, and the next day he was driven from the house. The rich man played the same trick on the fifth and sixth brothers. But when the seventh brother came by, the rich man was tired of his joke. He turned the dogs loose on the seventh brother.

The six other stupid brothers gathered around the bed of the seventh brother now wrapped in bandages from toe to chin. "Digit must die," they decided.

One night soon after, while their mother and wives slept, the brothers took Digit, pushed him into an *injera* basket, and carried him to the river. The brothers tied down the lid of the basket and threw it far out into the waters. They were certain that they would never see Digit again.

But the current of the river carried the basket along and washed it up on the shore. In the morning an Arab trader named Yusef found the basket and opened it. Out hopped Digit. He began to dance and sing, "Oh, you are lucky. You are Allah's favored son."

"Why am I lucky?" the Arab asked. "I have only found a wet, very little boy on a river bank. What is lucky about that?"

Digit said, "Do I look unusual or strange?"

"You are unusually tiny," Yusef said.

"Yes. I am very small," Digit agreed. "For that reason I am the messenger of Allah. But for my small size I could not have fitted into this magic basket. And what a magic basket this is! Each day at noon it fills with gold.''

Yusef was fascinated by a basket that filled with gold each day, but he was also greedy and worried. He said, "If I took the basket back to town, the governor would take it from me."

"That is true," Digit agreed. "That is why Allah sent it to this wilderness."

"I have an idea," Yusef said. "I will stay here until the basket fills with gold many times. I will load the gold onto mules. Then I will hide the basket up in those rocks. I can give the governor some of my gold and come back for more whenever I need it."

"You are wise," Digit said. "It is a pleasure to find a man who is not so overcome with greed that he stops thinking. Your plan sounds good. Where are your mules?"

The trader struck himself on the forehead and began to pull at his beard. "What do I say!" he wailed. "Fool, fool that I am! I sold my mules back at the last village and bought this fine horse to sell to the sheik Mustafa."

"Very well," Digit said. "I will stay with the basket and the gold. You ride your fine horse to the village and bring back mules."

"Oh, no," said the greedy Yusef. "I will stay with

the basket. You take this money and my horse and go for the mules. But you must tell no one about the magic basket.''

"I will tell no one," Digit promised. "But do not worry. Only a very stupid man would believe a story about a magic basket from a little boy.''

Yusef laughed. "That is true," he agreed. "No one would believe such a story. Go, and be quick about it."

Digit took the money from the trader and climbed hand-over-hand up the horse's tail and onto the saddle. "I must tell you one other thing," Digit said. "You are new to the basket. If it does not fill with gold at noon on the first day, do not worry. You must be patient. The gold is worth waiting for."

"I will be patient," Yusef promised. "There will be thousands of noons to come. The first one is just the beginning."

Digit left Yusef sitting in front of the basket, watching for the sun to reach the middle of the heavens. The horse was swift and strong, and Digit was at his home that night. Digit let all of his brothers see the horse and ride on it. But he would not tell them where he got the horse. He showed them the trader's money and told them he had had many horses and sold them to get the money.

Then Digit gave the money and the horse to his mother.

"Why do you giant fools never bring me money or horses?" the mother shouted at her other sons. "You bring me nothing but trouble. If it were not for the little one, we would all starve."

That night while the brothers filled the house with the rumble and thunder of their snoring, Digit crept to the bed of his oldest brother. To his brother Digit whispered, "I found the horses in the river where you threw me. There are many more there. Tomorrow while the others still sleep, we will go there. When I whistle it will be the signal to rise and go to the river."

Digit then crept to the bed of his next oldest brother. "I found the horses in the forest," he whispered. "I tell only you of this. Tomorrow we will go there. I will whistle. Rise and follow me to the forest."

Digit told the next brother that the horses were on the mountain. To the fourth, Digit said that he had found the horses by the lake. He told the next brother that he had found the horses on the desert. The sixth brother Digit told to go to the deep valley, and the last brother was to go to the meadow.

While the brothers were sleeping and dreaming of horses, Digit tied all of their legs together.

In the morning Digit gave a shrill whistle through a hollow tube. The brothers jumped out of their beds and began to run in seven different directions. Enraged because they were tied together, they began to strike out and kick at one another. Finally they beat each other senseless.

Later that day Digit said to his mother, "I will go after more horses."

"And where will you find them?" she asked.

"Wherever fools ride them," Digit told her.

There is no end to the Digit story. And no end to stories about Digit. In one series of stories Digit becomes a house burglar; he enters houses by riding underneath a cat. We must tell you that we found no story in which Digit reformed and became an honest little boy. You could say one thing for Digit, however. He was always good to his poor old mother.

# 6
# Lion Bones and the Gardula Magicians

We heard this story of lion bones in several parts of Ethiopia, and it may have been told first in India or Arabia. Good folk stories have always had a way of moving from one country to another and even from one continent to another. They are adapted to the culture they are being told in, but the idea or message remains the same. In the case of this funny little story the message is unmistakable: There *is* such a thing as being too clever for your own good.

An Amhara farmer went to the southwest in Gama-Gofa to look for good land. Near Gardula the land was fertile, but nobody planted crops there. The Gardula people were more interested in magic than in farming. They thought that anyone could be a good farmer but that only very wise and skilled men could be good magicians.

The Amhara farmer listened to many wonderful stories of magic and magicians. But always he said, "The greatest magic is God's magic. He turned the forest and plain into a garden for our father Adam. Why do you not practice that magic? Then I would marvel. Then I would admire you."

One day the farmer was walking through a forest, and he met three of the greatest magicians of Gardula. The great magicians said that the farmer could walk along behind them if he was quiet and did not try to talk. The farmer agreed to be silent. The Gardula magicians told many wonderful stories. Each tried to tell a more wonderful story than the others. As they walked through the forest, they came upon the bones of a lion. The bones had been picked clean by vultures, hyenas, and ants.

The first magician said, "Now watch closely, Farmer. I can put these lion bones together just as they once were." The magician bent down and put the bones together and formed the perfect skeleton of a lion.

"That was easy," the second magician said. "I can put flesh on these bones and make a real-looking lion." The magician did that.

"Wonderful," the farmer said. "But a lion is not a lion without his fierce spirit and his roar."

"Watch me," the third magician said. "I will

breathe a lion's spirit into this lifeless body. I will make the lion roar."

"And I will climb a tree," the farmer said.

The farmer climbed a tree, and the third magician breathed spirit into the lion.

The lion stood up, blinked, shook himself, roared—and ate the three magicians.

From the tree the farmer watched in awe and said, "Truly, the magicians of Gardula are very clever."

# 7
# The Wise Judge

The story which is about a trial or judgment is a type of folktale that we found in several parts of Ethiopia. The main character in such stories is usually a king or a judge. Sometimes the king or judge is shown to be a wise man—as in "The King's Black Curtain"—but in many stories he is made to look foolish. There is a good reason for this. Some Ethiopian kings, particularly in earlier times, were cruel and ruled with an iron hand. People resented and feared such kings, but to speak out against them was dangerous; protest could result in punishment or even death. An old Ethiopian proverb says, "The sky cannot be plowed nor a king questioned." In other words, speaking out against a king is as foolish as trying to farm in the clouds.

But one safe way that the people could protest against injustice was through stories about kings and judges. Such stories changed the names and places and poked fun at or criticized the king and his judges. Judges appeared in these stories because they were appointed by the king; they were his agents.

We heard many king and judge stories from the Oromo people in central and western Ethiopia. The Oromo (whom the Amhara call "Galla") migrated from the Rift Valley lowlands to the Ethiopian highlands over three hundred years ago and came into immediate conflict with the ruling Amhara. The Oromo persisted, however, and today are the largest ethnic group in Ethiopia. Sometimes the Oromo and Amhara have come together to fight a common enemy. In 1896, the Oromo joined the Amhara and other Ethiopian groups and, led by Emperor Menelik II, inflicted a crushing defeat on the Italian invaders at the Battle of Adowa in Tigray Province. But for the most part no love has been lost between the Oromo and the Amhara.

The following story, one of the funniest we heard in our two years in Ethiopia, was told to us one night by an old Oromo farmer.

The good widow Yemswitch, who many years ago had lost most of her hearing, had now lost all of her sheep. The whole flock had wandered off while she was washing clothes at the river, and she had not the least idea where they had gone. She set out looking for them and soon met the good farmer Mulugeta, who had just finished his day's plowing.

"*Ato* Mulugeta," said Yemswitch, "have you seen my sheep anywhere today?"

Now it so happened that Mulugeta was also hard of hearing—if anything, deafer than Yemswitch. He always had to guess at what a person was saying. Since he had just come from his field, he guessed that the good widow was asking about his work.

"Yes, *Woizero* Yemswitch," he answered, "I have worked hard today."

He pointed toward his plowed field to show her how much he had done. Yemswitch, however, did not hear a word that he said. She thought that he was pointing to where he had seen her sheep.

"Thank you, Farmer Mulugeta," she said. "If I find my sheep over there, I shall give you one of them."

They bowed politely to each other, and Yemswitch went looking for her sheep in the direction that Mulugeta had pointed. As luck would have it, she found the sheep in a little grove of trees just over the hill. She was very grateful to the good farmer for having been so careful to watch which way her sheep were going. Had she not found them before dark, the jackals or a leopard certainly would have got them.

Yemswitch discovered that one of the lambs had a

badly injured leg, and she decided to give that lamb to Mulugeta. She went to his house and found him preparing his own supper, for his wife had been dead for many years.

"*Ato* Mulugeta," Yemswitch said, "I have found my sheep exactly where you said they were. I have brought you this fine lamb for a reward."

Mulugeta heard nothing that she said, but he saw that the lamb had an injured leg. He thought that Yemswitch was accusing him of hurting the lamb.

"Oh, no," he said firmly. "I had nothing to do with that. Why should I hurt your lamb?"

Yemswitch, who heard clearly only the word "no," thought that Mulugeta wanted a better sheep for his reward. "You are a greedy man," she said. "All you did was point the direction the sheep had gone. Here, take this lamb or none at all."

She tried to put the lamb in his arms, but he refused to take it. "I will not pay for this lamb," he said. "I had nothing to do with its accident."

They fell to arguing and calling each other names, but of course that made little difference since neither of them heard one-tenth of what the other said. They made so much noise, however, that a policeman heard them and insisted that they go to a judge to settle their quarrel.

The policeman took them to the court of Justice

Yasu Wolde-Johannas, an elderly judge who had been appointed many years ago by the king. Justice Yasu was famous throughout the land for the fairness and wisdom of his court decisions. It might seem strange that Justice Yasu could be so wise and fair in deciding cases brought before him, for the truth was that he could scarcely hear a word that was said, even when shouted. But the good man was also nearly blind, and so he would not judge people on how they looked, as almost everyone does. That made him a very fair judge.

The widow Yemswitch told her side of the case first. She pointed to the lamb which she still held. "My reward was generous," she shouted. "*Ato* Mulugeta is a greedy man to want more."

Mulugeta then explained at great length that he was a kind man who would never think of hurting a little lamb. "I was busy in my field all day," he said, also shouting. "I had not even seen the animal until she accused me."

Justice Yasu listened carefully to the shouting, though he heard nothing, and peered intently at the two people before him. Finally, he made out that they were an old man and an old woman. The woman, he decided, was holding a child in her arms. The judge had had much experience with the troubles of people. He decided that this man and woman wanted to get a divorce. They wanted him to decide which one should keep the child.

"How many years have you been married?" the judge asked.

Yemswitch, listening carefully, thought that the judge had asked her how many sheep she had.

"Twenty, Your Worship," she shouted at the top of her voice.

Justice Yasu heard this answer, and he at once reached his decision. "I am ashamed of you both," he said. "You have been married for twenty years and still have not learned to live together. My decision is that you must continue to live together and to make a good home for this little child. And if you do not do this, I shall put you both in prison. That is all. The case is dismissed."

The officers of the court finally made Yemswitch and Mulugeta understand the decision of Justice Yasu.

"But how can we live together?" wailed Yemswitch. "We are not married."

"Then you had better get married," the bailiff told her. "The good judge will surely put you into prison if you do not carry out his order."

So the widow Yemswitch and the farmer Mulugeta went to a priest and were married that night. Since Yemswitch was a very good cook and Mulugeta was a very good farmer—and since neither of them could ever hear what the other was saying—they lived happily ever afterward.

And the fame of the wise judge, Justice Yasu Wolde-Johannas, spread even farther through the land.

# 8
# King Firdy the Just

The previous story is a comedy, but its purpose is not to make fun of the characters because of their physical disabilities. They are presented sympathetically and shown to be good people. Their deafness and blindness are used to make an amusing comment about how the king's agents sometimes arrived at "justice." The tone of the following story, however, is anything but comic. It is a bitter, intensely satiric picture of a king who turns justice upside down.

In the western lands of Ethiopia there once lived a great king known as King Firdy the Just. He prided himself on the fairness with which he judged the cases that were brought before him. No one in the country had ever been heard to say a word against the decisions that King Firdy reached. That was a good thing because the king had long ago decreed that anyone who spoke against him would be roasted over a slow fire.

One night in the king's city a thief named Asrat tried to break into the home of a wealthy merchant by digging a hole through a wall of the man's house. Just when the hole was big enough, however, a brick fell out of the wall and hit Asrat on the head. It was really a nasty blow, and the thief had to stagger away with only a bloody head and a big bump for his night's work.

Asrat was very angry at what had happened, and the next morning he went to the palace of King Firdy the Just to complain. "Last night, O King," he said, "I was breaking into the house of the merchant Paulos to steal a few trifling things. But a brick fell out of the wall and hit me on the head. Look, you can still see the bump. I was too badly hurt to continue my work. Someone should be punished for this."

King Firdy looked at the bump, and his voice shook with rage when he spoke. "You are right," he shouted. "What has this country come to when a thief cannot break into a house without risking accidents of this kind?" The king turned to his guards and said, "Bring the merchant Paulos to me."

The merchant was brought, and he was trembling with fear. Everyone stood in terror of the justice of King Firdy. "Merchant," said the king, "this good thief was injured while trying to break into your house. Since it was your house, it is my judgment that you are to blame."

"O King," said the merchant in a quaking voice, "it is true that it was my house. But the person to blame is really the carpenter who built the house for me. He must have built the house badly. That is why the brick fell."

"Perhaps you are right," said the king. "Bring the carpenter to me. My only desire is to punish the guilty person."

The carpenter was brought before King Firdy. The king said, "You wretched man! Do you know that the good thief Asrat has been injured because of careless work you did on the house of the merchant Paulos? A brick fell and struck poor Asrat on the head while he was digging through the wall."

The carpenter was nearly fainting from fear, but he managed to say, "O King, it is true that I built the house. But the bricks were put in by the stonemason Felleke. It is he who should be punished."

"Bring the stonemason Felleke to me," said King Firdy, "and I will see that justice is done."

So the stonemason was brought before King Firdy. When the king accused him of causing the injury to the thief Asrat, Felleke whispered in terror, "O good King, it is not I who should be punished for the injury to the thief. The man who sold me the mortar to hold the bricks together was Kebede Gabre. If the mortar had been good, the brick would not have fallen on the thief's head. It is Kebede who should be punished.''

Kebede was brought before King Firdy and the king said, "Hear, you wretched man, you who made the mortar that held together the bricks that were used to build the house of the merchant Paulos. While trying to steal a few trifling things, the good thief Asrat was struck on the head by one of these bricks. The brick must have come loose because of poor mortar. You shall be punished severely for this."

Unfortunately, Kebede was a huge oaf of a man who had great strength but little brain. He could think of nothing to say in his defense. King Firdy—sure that he had found the guilty man—commanded that a gallows be built and that Kebede be hanged at once.

The carpenters built the gallows hastily, however, and they did not build the structure high enough. Kebede was an extremely tall man. When the guards took him to the gallows to hang him, they found that when the rope was around his neck, his feet still touched the ground.

The guards reported this problem to King Firdy the Just, and the king was terribly angry. "How much longer is the wrong that was done to the good thief Asrat to go unpunished?" he shouted. "A gallows has been built, and someone must be punished!"

So the guards went out, and the first man they met was a little onion farmer who had just come to town to sell his crop. It was well known that this little farmer was a good man who had never harmed anyone. But he was small and so would fit the gallows perfectly. King Firdy was inside his palace crying for justice.

When the farmer was taken before King Firdy, the king shouted, "Yes! Yes! He will do perfectly. The good thief has waited long enough for justice."

So the little onion farmer was taken to the gallows. He fitted it very well, and justice was done in the land of King Firdy.

# 9
# The Ant and the Tower to God

This story from the Gurage people, who live south and west of Addis Ababa, is about a king, but it is not a "king story" as the previous ones about kings have been. This is a story about the danger of vanity and self-importance, and it is a good illustration of the old adage that "pride goeth before a fall."

The story is a good reflection of the Gurage themselves. They are a humble, hard-working people; in fact, the word for laborer in many parts of Ethiopia is "gurage." Gurage men travel all over Ethiopia to find work on coffee plantations, on road-building crews, and even on the docks of Red Sea ports such as Assab and Masswa. When they have saved enough money, they come back to Gurage country and buy farms with the money they have made.

With its baboon characters and its subtle message that the most humble of God's creatures (meaning people) have a right to be heard, "The Ant and the Tower to God" is one of the purest African folktales.

A great baboon king once ruled over the land of baboons with such wisdom and justice that all baboons loved him greatly. Even the smaller and less intelligent creatures loved the baboon king. They wanted him to be their king too. But the baboons would not permit this.

"Why do ants and worms and other little things need a wise baboon as their king?" they asked. "They are not great animals. This is our king."

After many years the king grew old and sick and finally died. All of the baboons wept and wailed at the loss of their great king. But they forbade other animals to weep for him.

"He was our king," they told the others. "Only we have the right to cry for him."

The baboons gathered to have a great funeral feast. All the baboon chiefs gave speeches praising the virtues of their departed leader. After much crying and more speeches, one chief rose and said, "We must do something wonderful for our great king. His memory must be held high. What is the greatest honor we can pay him now that he is dead?"

One wise old chief answered, "We can take his body directly up to God. That would be a great honor."

"How can we do that?" the others asked. "God is in heaven. How can we get up there?"

"If we all work together very hard, we can do it," the old baboon said. "Anything is possible for creatures who have hands. We can build a tower to God."

The baboons set to work to build their tower to God. But everything they used to build the tower crumbled. The wood split, and the stones tumbled down. The wise old baboon said, "We must put ourselves into this. Other things will not do. We must bring all of the baboons of the world together. Then we can build a tower to God with our very bodies. One baboon can get on the back of another, and so on until our baboon tower reaches to heaven."

The baboons from all the world were gathered. They climbed, one on top of another, and the tower began to reach up toward heaven.

Now a small ant had been traveling from a distant land to mourn for the king of baboons. He had not heard that this was forbidden to small creatures. The ant arrived at the place where the baboon tower was almost built. The ant tried to call up to a big baboon who was about to climb up and form the top of the tower. He wanted to ask how he could join in the mourning.

"Sir," the ant called. "Sir, one moment please."

But the big baboon ignored him. The baboon felt

very important. He was going to form the top of the tower. He did not have time for a silly little ant.

The ant walked over to the wise old baboon who was supervising the building of the baboon tower. "Sir," the ant cried, to try to get his attention.

But the wise old baboon was too busy to talk to him. "Climb! Climb!" he called to the last baboon. "We are almost up to heaven."

Finally, the ant walked over to the base of the baboon tower. He saw the feet of the great baboon who formed the base of the tower. This baboon was a huge and powerful fellow who held up all the other baboons on his shoulders. The ant knew that his own little voice would not carry up to this mighty baboon.

So, to get the attention of the huge baboon, the ant stung him on the foot. The baboon gave a great cry and a great jump, and the whole tower crumpled and fell to the ground with a crash.

As baboons tumbled down all around him, the ant said as loudly as he could, "I came to tell you that I am sorry about the death of your great king."

# 10
# The Lion's Share

*Danakil!* This word once struck fear into the hearts of people over much of Ethiopia. The Danakil are nomads who wander over the hot, arid desert of northeastern Ethiopia; their movements are restricted only by the necessity of staying close to permanent water wells. The Danakil have long had the reputation of being the most ferocious tribe in the whole of the horn of Africa. All of the peoples whose lands border the desert—the Tigray, the Oromo, the Somali, the Adira—once knew the terror of a Danakil raid at night. These wandering warriors raided for cattle and camels; sometimes for revenge; sometimes for the sheer love of fighting. Raiding is now largely a thing of the past, but the Danakil are still a fiercely proud people and consider themselves superior to all other tribes. Although they are known as Danakil to other Ethiopians, their name for themselves in their own language is *Afar,* which means "the Only People."

You would expect Danakil stories to deal with fighting and the importance of being strong, and they do. In the following story the old lion is, of course, the Danakil, and the hyenas are all of the other tribes. And there is no mistaking the point of the story: to the strong goes everything.

In the Batie foothills where they slope down to the flat Danakil plain, there lived an old hyena and his nine sons. Although the old one was in good health, he preferred to stay in their cave day and night—to guard it, so he said—and send his sons out to hunt for food. Still, he took his duties as a father seriously, for he talked to his sons constantly about what a brave hunter and strong-hearted fighter he was. He made clear that he expected his sons to follow in his footsteps.

One evening the nine sons went out together on their nightly search for food. They had not gone far through the underbrush when they were unexpectedly joined by a great tawny-maned lion who lived in the neighborhood. The hyenas were about to slink away by themselves when the lion stopped them.

"Just a minute, friends," he said. "Why don't we hunt together? I have been searching for two hours and haven't found a thing. With your sense of smell and my strength, we might get something good. Then we will split our catch."

The hyenas would have been much happier by themselves, but since none of them wanted to say no to the lion, they went along with him. Luck was with them, for almost immediately the hyenas' sharp noses led them to a tree where a hunter had tied a bag of freshly killed guinea hens, expecting to return for them later. He had not tied them quite high enough, however, for by stretching to his full length the big lion was able to pull the bag down.

They tore it open eagerly and pulled out the guinea hens. Ten birds were in the bag. "You see how wise it was for us to hunt together," the lion said. "Now we shall share the food."

He selected nine of the fattest guinea hens for himself. The one undersized bird that was left he tossed to the hyenas. All nine hyenas howled in protest, and the lion frowned slightly at the noise.

"What's the matter?" he asked, looking at each hyena in turn. "Didn't I divide them right?"

The hyenas were afraid to answer him, so the lion picked up the nine fat guinea hens and walked off toward his den. The unhappy hyenas, knowing that their father would scold them if they did not return soon with food, picked up their thin little bird and re-turned to their cave.

When the father saw the miserable night's haul, he made an angry speech about lazy, inconsiderate sons. "And do you really expect me to make a meal out of this mouthful of feathers?" he asked scornfully.

"Father," said one of the sons, "we had a very fine dinner for you, but the lion's share was bigger than we thought it would be." The son then told how they had hunted with the lion and how he had divided the guinea hens.

The old hyena was beside himself with rage, even before his son had finished. He called all of his sons cowards, weaklings, and ingrates. Then he turned his angry words against the lion and worked himself into such a frenzy that his sons were afraid he would fall into a fit.

At last his anger was so great that he quite forgot himself. Picking up the guinea hen, he started out of the cave, saying to his sons, "Follow me. I will go to that lion and exchange this insult for our fair share of the birds. I will see that justice is done. Be glad your father is brave."

They reached the lion's den, and the old hyena called out, "Ho, Lion! I want to talk to you."

There was a moment's silence. Then from inside

the den, the lion, who had apparently been sleeping off the effects of his feast, let out a great roar. He walked slowly out of his den and looked down at the hyena. His great mane stood up, and he was a picture of sheer power in the bright moonlight.

"Well, Friend Hyena," he said softly. "Do you want something?"

The old hyena gulped, cleared his throat, and picked up the guinea hen. "Why, Friend Lion," he said meekly, "my sons have told me how you shared your food with them. You were much too generous. We have come to present you with the tenth bird."

# 11
# Know Your Own Strength

We heard this story of a donkey who thought he could frighten a lion from a Danakil storyteller. We thought it was amusing, but it did not seem quite like other Danakil stories we had heard. (Compare it with "The Lion's Share.") The Danakil storyteller admitted that he had heard the donkey and rooster story long ago from a Gurage traveler. "I liked it," the Danakil storyteller said, "so I took it." It is just in this way that folktales move from one region and one people to another.

On a farm near the Awash River there lived a donkey and a rooster who were great friends. Now this might seem to you a strange friendship, but there were good reasons for it. The donkey was a meek little fellow who had carried heavy loads all his life. He had been worked so hard that he had never had a chance to drowse in the sun and talk, which he dearly loved to do. Now that he was old and not used much for packing things to market, his greatest pleasure was to walk lazily in the sunny meadow, occasionally pluck some tender grass, and talk about all manner of things, such as why there is so much sand in the desert and what makes stars shine.

Although the rooster did not know much about these weighty subjects, he had a good voice and enjoyed answering the donkey at great length. The donkey seemed to admire his rooster friend's knowledge very much. More important, the rooster was a lazy sort of fellow, and during those long talks in the meadow he rode on the donkey's back—which the donkey did not mind at all since he had carried much heavier loads all his life. Whenever the rooster spied a fat worm or a tasty bug, he would flap down, gobble it up, then fly again to the donkey's back. Thus he managed to stay well fed all the time, without having to do all the walking around that most of the other roosters on the farm had to do.

All in all it was a pleasant arrangement, and there never were two closer friends anywhere—until the day they met the lion. It was evening. They had fallen into a deep discussion about why water is always wet and had not noticed the setting sun.

From a nearby clump of bushes, a lion had been

watching the donkey for some time. When the donkey came close, the lion slipped from the bushes and padded silently toward him. When the donkey saw the lion, he was so frightened that he stopped and stood frozen, unable to lift so much as one foot. The lion was almost on him when for the first time he saw the rooster riding on the donkey's back. The rooster spied the lion at the same moment and crowed in terror and flapped his wings.

Instantly, the lion whirled around and ran back into the bushes. He knew that if the rooster kept crowing and flapping his wings, the farmer in the nearby house would hear him and come running with his gun. The old lion was much too smart to risk getting shot, just for a meal of one skinny donkey.

When the lion disappeared, the donkey slowly got over his fright, and then he became quite amazed. "Did you see that lion run away?" he said to the rooster. "I just stood here bravely, and he became afraid of me!"

The rooster was not quite so sure. "Do you really think the lion was afraid of you?" he asked doubtfully.

The donkey became very angry at his friend's doubts. He shook the rooster off his back. "Look," he said, "I don't think you'd better ride on me any more, and I'm afraid I won't have time to talk to you after this. I have more important things to do than talk. I have to guard this farm for my master."

The rooster was very sorry to lose his good friend, and he walked slowly back to the farmyard by himself. All the next day, the donkey went around the farm telling the different animals how the lion had been afraid of him. Toward evening, after having told his story at least fifty times, the donkey trotted off toward the bushes at the edge of the meadow. He thought it was about time to frighten the lion again.

The lion was waiting for him, and this time he made sure there was no rooster on the donkey's back. He crept out of the bushes, making not a sound but coming forward with a deadly purpose. The donkey saw him and snorted and kicked up his heels, but the lion only came faster toward him.

"Ho, Lion," said the donkey. "I'm the brave donkey who frightened you last night. You'd better get away."

The lion did not answer but instead kept on coming. When the lion was almost on him, the donkey realized that something had gone wrong. He turned tail and ran with all his speed for the farmyard; but while he was a good runner, he was no match for the lion. The lion sprang at him and that would have been the end, except for a very lucky thing. At that moment the donkey stepped into a hole and went sprawling on the ground, turning head over heels. The lion sailed right over him without so much as touching him.

The donkey finished his somersault on his feet and kept right on running. The lion, however, landed on a big rock, and his breath was knocked completely out of him. By the time he got up, the donkey was all the way back to the farmyard. Again the lion had no intention of risking a bullet from the farmer and disappeared into the bushes.

The rooster was perched up in a tree and had seen everything that had happened. As the donkey walked to the tree and lay down wearily, the rooster fluttered down on his back. The rooster was really very glad to have his friend back, but he couldn't help saying something just a bit mean.

"Well, my friend," he said. "I think we had better talk about how important it is not to think that you are stronger than you really are."

The donkey nodded and closed his eyes. He was very, very tired. "Yes," he said, "I agree. But let's talk about it tomorrow. And you might be thinking about why it gets so dark at night. We'll talk about that, too."

# 12
# Saint Gabre Manfas and His Animals

Probably the stories best known to most Ethiopians and most loved by them are religious stories. There are hundreds of them, and they are told in pictures on the walls and ceilings of churches all over the country. Whether the pictures were painted long ago or more recently, they are all painted in bright colors and in a so-called primitive flat style, without depth. Many of the stories are famous ones from the Bible: the life of Jesus, Adam and Eve, Salome and John the Baptist, Noah's Ark. One of the most popular scenes is that of Saint George slaying the dragon; Saint George is considered to be the patron saint of Ethiopia.

Many of the pictures tell religious stories that are unknown to the rest of the Christian world. In its centuries of isolation during the Middle Ages, Ethiopia developed its own stories of Christian saints and sinners and marvelous events. There is the story of Tekle-Haimanot, the most beloved of Ethiopian saints, who prayed for seven years without sleep. He stood on one leg to keep himself awake and ate nothing but seven grains of wheat during the entire seven years. There is the story of the girl who fell in love with the devil and went to live with him in hell; and there is the story—told to us by the old monk bird watcher—of the holy man who burned the waters of the lake Haik in order to show the sinful lake people the power of the Lord. The following story of Saint Gabre Manfas is typical of Ethiopia's many religious legends.

Long ago in Ethiopia a very religious woman gave birth to a baby boy. The baby looked normal and healthy, but his parents were greatly worried because he would drink no milk, not even his mother's, nor would he eat any of the soft foods made of bread crumbs or cereal. The only thing that the baby would take was water. Yet he lived and grew strong and healthy as any other little boy in the village.

A year passed, and then two and three, but never did Gabre Manfas, for such was the boy's name, take anything but water. By that time Gabre's parents realized that their child must be especially blessed by God. There was no other way to explain how he could live on nothing but water. Soon all of the people in the country round about knew that God had sent a saint to live in their midst, and religious men and women from all parts of the country made pilgrimages to the boy's home.

As the young saint grew up, he continued to take nothing but water, and he spent most of his time reading the holy books and praying. He did not play with the other children, and he avoided grown-ups, even his own parents. When he was not praying or reading, he preferred to roam in the forests and talk to the animals. He had no fear, even of the leopards or lions, and all wild animals followed him unafraid.

One day a farmer and his son were driving a cow and a sheep to a town near Gabre Manfas's birthplace. They wished to present the animals to the town's priests for the feast that was held each year on Saint Tekle-Haimanot's birthday. Near the town, however, they met a lion and a leopard, and both father and son ran away leaving the cow and sheep behind. The lion and leopard took these two animals to Gabre Manfas, who was in the forest nearby, and asked the saint what should be done with them.

Gabre Manfas said, "Take the cow and sheep deep into the forest and feed them well for a year. Then on Saint Tekle-Haimanot's next birthday take them to the town and give them to the head priest. The good farmer brought them for the glory of God, and for that purpose they should be used."

The lion and leopard did as Gabre Manfas wished. They took the cow and sheep to a part of the forest where the grass was best and the water purest, and they watched over them day and night for a year.

At the end of the year the lion and leopard drove the cow and the sheep into the village and took them to the church. All of the townspeople fled in terror when they saw the fierce jungle cats. Even the young priests fled. But the head priest was unafraid. When he saw the lion and leopard sitting patiently tending the sheep and cow, he knew that they must have been sent by Saint Gabre Manfas himself. Then the townspeople and young priests came back, and they were amazed at the size of the two animals that had been brought to celebrate the religious feast day that honors Saint Tekle-Haimanot.

When he grew older, Gabre Manfas set out on a long journey. He traveled all over the country, and the animals he had known in the forest near his village went with him. As they walked through the land, other animals followed him, and he talked to all of them and was kind to them.

Once they came to a burning, waterless desert, and they were all tortured with thirst. They came upon a small black bird lying on the hot sands, its wings spread out, its beak open in agony. The bird begged Gabre Manfas to give it just one drop of water.

The saint was overcome with pity for the bird. "I have not even one drop of water," he said. "But you may drink from the tears of my eyes."

The bird did so, and from that time on it flew with Gabre Manfas wherever the saint might go. In church pictures that tell the story of Saint Gabre Manfas, you will always find the scene of the bird drinking from the saint's eyes.

Many years passed, and Gabre Manfas became a very old man. At last the Lord sent his angel to tell the saint to prepare for death. Gabre Manfas was sad.

"I would like to live to take care of my animals," he said. "Who else shall care for them?"

The angel returned and told God of the saint's desire to stay on earth, and God let him live. After another hundred years, God sent his angel again to Saint Gabre Manfas, and the angel told him to prepare for death.

"But my animals," said Saint Gabre. "They are still with me. I have never eaten any living thing, either plant or animal, and therefore I have not sinned. For this reason I should not have to die."

Once more God let Gabre Manfas remain on earth, but after another hundred years, he sent the angel to the saint.

"Will you not come with me and sit on the right of God's throne in heaven?" the angel asked.

Then Gabre Manfas knew that God must want him

very much, so he said goodbye to his beloved animals and left them for his place in heaven.

When church artists paint the story of Saint Gabre Manfas, they do not show him sitting on the right of God's throne. They always picture him wandering on earth with his animals.

# 13
# King Solomon and the Queen of Sheba

The Beta Israel are a small but fascinating Ethiopian ethnic group who live in the northwestern part of the country near Lake Tana, Ethiopia's largest lake and the source of the Blue Nile River. The Beta Israel (their name means "Those of the House of Israel") are Jews. They are called Falashas by other Ethiopians, but the Beta Israel do not like that name because *falasha* means "stranger" in the Amharic language. The Beta Israel do not think of themselves as strangers. They have lived in Ethiopia and followed many of the traditions of Judaism for longer than there is any historical record. The six-pointed Star of David marks the huts that serve as their synagogues. They observe Passover and the Day of Atonement.

When did Judaism come to Ethiopia? When did the Beta Israel become Jews? Historians and biblical scholars simply do not know. Some scholars think they began with a "lost tribe" of Israelites that became separated from the main group when Moses led the Jews out of Egypt three thousand years ago. Some say the Beta Israel were converted by Jewish traders at a later date but still long ago. But no one really knows. The Beta Israel are the mystery people of Ethiopia.

The Beta Israel have their own answer to this question. They say that they came to Ethiopia in the time of King Solomon. They say they came with the Queen of Sheba when she returned to Ethiopia after a trip to Israel. The legend of the Queen of Sheba and Solomon is one of the most ancient and best-loved stories in Ethiopia. Here is the way the black Jews of Ethiopia tell it.

Solomon, the great and wise, ruled over Israel a thousand years before the birth of Christ. Solomon by wisdom and hard work extended his rule over land that stretched from the ancient city of Babylon to the ancient land of Egypt. From his capital in Israel, Solomon sent ships through the Mediterranean and through the Red Sea. The merchants on those ships spread the fame of Solomon, wisest and richest of ancient kings.

When Solomon ruled over Israel, the Queen of Sheba ruled over the highlands of eastern Africa. When she heard of the wisdom, riches, and power of the great

Solomon, she wished to visit the mightiest king of her time. She made up a great caravan and loaded it with gold, precious jewels, spices, and rich cloth. Then with many soldiers and slaves, she set out for Israel, the land of Solomon.

The journey to Israel took many months. When the queen came to the court of Solomon, he was stunned by her beauty, wisdom, and goodness. He fell in love with her and invited her to stay in the royal palace. She could not refuse for fear of offending the king.

One night Solomon came to the chambers where the queen slept and urged her to stay always in Israel. But she refused. Solomon then said that he would bother her no more if she would agree not to take anything in his palace except what he, himself, gave her. To this she agreed. Sheba was very rich, and she saw no need for any of Solomon's treasures. She agreed to stay in Israel if she took anything without his permission.

The next night Solomon sent many trays of rich and heavily spiced food to the queen's chambers. He came to dine with her. During the dinner he urged her to try dish after dish of the rich and peppery food. After dinner, Solomon rose and went back to his own quarters. As he left he cautioned, "Touch not the most common object without my permission."

In the middle of the night, Sheba awoke with a great thirst, but the wily Solomon had sent no water to her chambers. She crept out of her bedroom and took a jar of water from another room. She drank the water.

At that moment Solomon entered her bedroom. He said that she had broken her promise and had taken something without his permission. "Even though you took the most common object rather than the most precious, this object was not given to you. Therefore, you have broken your promise."

Since Sheba had broken her promise, she had to stay in the court of Solomon; and his love for her beauty, wisdom, and goodness grew. But her people wished her to return to Ethiopia. Since she was their queen, she felt that it was her duty to return.

Finally, Sheba convinced Solomon that she must go home. He showered her with riches and great gifts for the journey. In her caravan Solomon put the finest young men chosen from the tribes of Israel. Back in Ethiopia, a child—the son of Solomon—was born to Sheba. She named him Menelik and raised him in the religion of the Israelites. He became Ethiopia's first truly great king.

From that time on, all Ethiopian rulers had to be able to convince their subjects that they had the blood of King Solomon and the Queen of Sheba in their veins. Although historical evidence was of course lacking, Emperor Haile Selassie claimed to be 225th in the long line of imperial descendants from the biblical ancestors. And the Beta Israel have always claimed that they are the descendants of the young Israelites sent by Solomon to guard his beloved Sheba.

# 14
# The Gift and the Giver

**M**ost of the stories we heard in Beta Israel country were based on the Old Testament of the Bible. But not all. The following story, told to us one night by an old Beta Israel storyteller, was one of our very special favorites from all of our travels in Ethiopia.

Once a poor farmer found a beautiful apple growing on a tree in his field. The apple was so large, so shiny, and so well-shaped that the farmer cried with joy when he saw it. Never had he seen such a beautiful apple on any tree in his country.

The farmer picked the apple, wrapped it in his cloak, and brought it to his home. He showed it to his wife and daughter, and they were as amazed as he to see such a beautiful apple.

Other farmers who lived in that village heard

about the apple and came to see it. They, too, agreed that it was a wondrous apple. They touched it tenderly and said that it was a beautiful apple, shaped to perfection by the hand of God.

After everyone had admired the apple, the question came—what to do with it? The farmer wished to give it to his daughter. He said to her, "Truly, this is the only thing that matches you in beauty. On both the fruit and your face, the work of God's hand is clear. Take the apple and eat of it."

But the daughter was too modest. She said she was not worthy of such a wonderful thing. She urged her father to take the apple for himself. It was given to him as a sign of God's love and blessings. "It is worthy of a king," the daughter said.

"You are right," the farmer agreed. "Such a fruit is worthy of a king. It is the only gift that I, a poor farmer, can give that will be worthy of my king."

The farmer's wife wrapped the apple in the finest cloth she had, and the farmer set out for the royal city. He carried the fruit very carefully in the cloth, and he walked along the road slowly. After many days, he reached the city, but the poor farmer could not get in to see the king. The guards at the palace laughed at him and kept him out.

"The king has thousands of fruit trees," they said.

"Surely your apple can be no more beautiful than those of the king."

The farmer opened the cloth and asked the guards to look. The apple was still as beautiful as the day it had been picked. Finally a guard went away to call the commander. The commander of the guard admired the apple and decided that he would bring the farmer to the chambers of the king.

When the farmer came before the king, he spoke in this way: "Your Majesty, Great King, beloved of us all, I have found a most beautiful apple on one of the trees of my field. It was such a wondrous fruit that men came from miles around to see it. I decided that only our beloved king could deserve this apple, and I have carried it to you."

The king was greatly moved by the simple love of the farmer. "What would you have from me in return?" he asked.

The farmer was greatly surprised. He said, "I want nothing, Your Majesty, but to see the joy on your face when you see this apple that God has made."

The farmer opened the cloth and handed the apple to the king. The king looked at it and said, "It is surely a work of God's hand. Such size. Such color. It shines like a bright jewel."

The king called the queen and all of his family,

and they too marveled at the beautiful apple. While people of the palace were admiring the apple, the poor farmer left the court and started for home. The king noticed that he was gone.

"Where is the farmer?" he asked. "He has shown me more love with this gift than anyone in the kingdom. Ride after him. Take my best horse and give it to him. Tell him the horse is from a grateful king who has learned a new lesson in kindness."

The servants rode after the farmer and found him plodding along the road. The farmer was overjoyed with the gift, which he had not expected. He rode away happily toward his village.

Word travels fast in a palace. Soon all the people in the royal city learned that the king had given his best horse to a poor farmer in exchange for a mere piece of fruit.

A rich merchant of the city heard the story of the king's gift. The merchant began to scheme. He thought, That poor farmer gave the king a simple apple. And the king gave him his best horse in exchange. What would the king give me if I gave him a fine horse? He might give me his daughter. Or perhaps some valuable jewels!

The merchant picked the best horse from his stable and led it up to the gates of the palace. "I have a gift for the king," the merchant told the guards. The guards let him in at once.

The merchant went before the king. "I have heard that you gave your own horse to a farmer," the merchant said. "For that reason, I have brought you a fine horse from my stable."

"Thank you very much," the king said.

The merchant moved restlessly, first standing on one foot then on the other. The merchant stroked his beard and looked worried. "Did you want something of me?" the king asked. The merchant stared down at the floor and did not meet the king's eyes.

"Ah, I see," the king said. "You have given me a gift. Now you expect something in return. Very well. Wait here."

The king left the room. The merchant could hardly hide his joy. It will be jewels, he thought. The king has gone to get jewels. I'm sure it will be jewels.

The king returned carrying something wrapped in a rich cloth. "Take this apple," the king said to the merchant. "It is most precious to me because it was given by a man who expected nothing in return. But you may have it."

The rich merchant was stunned. He opened up the cloth and saw the perfection of the apple, but he paid no attention to its beauty. The merchant walked angrily out of the palace. When he was outside, he threw the apple away. He began to pull at his beard and wail in a loud voice.

The king ordered his guards to drive the merchant from the palace grounds. "Tell him," the king said, "that a gift is only as good as the heart of the giver. A person should give without expecting a gift in return. Any other gift is of no value."

The king looked at the beautiful horse the merchant had brought him. "This horse is worthless as a gift," he said. "As something to ride on, however, it seems to be a very fine horse."

# 15
# The Three Suitors

Onc of the storytellers we met in our travels was a Somali camel driver. We met him in Jigjigga, the main Somali town in Ethiopia, where the wind seems always to blow off the hot, arid lowland plain. The wind carries fine dust, and the Somalis wrap their cloaks about their faces to keep from breathing it. When people talk in the big open market at Jigjigga, they often squat and speak from behind their cloaks.

We visited the market to meet the camel driver, who we had been told knew many stories. We found him squatting against the mud wall of a building, drinking hot tea. The wind drove sand and dust everywhere, but we drank tea and talked with the camel driver for a long time. The Somalis are fond of stories that are puzzles or riddles. Here is one of the stories that the camel driver told us.

Three men were in love with the same woman. All three men were of equal rank and wealth. All three men asked for the girl's hand in marriage.

You would think that such a thing would gladden the heart of the girl's father. But it did not. Instead of being glad, the father's heart was full of grief. No matter how he chose, he was sure to offend two of the country's most powerful men. Of course, the girl herself had no choice, nor did she say which of the three she loved. So the father had to worry alone.

Each day the fathers of the three young men urged the father of the girl to make a choice. But each day the girl's father put them off. He consulted the great holy men of the country, and he looked in the holy book, the Koran, but he found no answer to his problem. If he chose one of the young men, the other two fathers were sure to be angry, and he did not want powerful men angry at him.

Finally, the father decided that he would have a test of skill to determine the young man who would win his daughter's hand. Three of the oldest and wisest men of the village were chosen to judge the contest. Each young man was to do whatever he wished to demonstrate his skill.

The first young man was the strongest of the three. He hoisted two heavy men on his shoulders and swam across the river and back. The village people cheered this great feat of strength.

The second young man was very skillful with a rifle. He shot sticks out of the teeth of his friends. He pierced a silver coin with a bullet as it spun through the air. The villagers marveled at this great marksmanship.

The third young man could play a harp and sing with a beauty that never before had been heard. His music could make birds pause in flight and wild animals stop their fearful cries to listen. He played his harp and sang for the contest. All of the village maidens sighed and smiled behind their veils. All of the young village men grew angry.

After the third suitor had performed, the wise old judges went to a coffeehouse to make their decision. And what was their decision? Did it help the father of the girl make his decision? Finally, after much coffee and much talking they announced that they had made their decision. This is what they decided:

The first young man had performed the greatest feats of strength. The second young man had performed the greatest feats of skill with a rifle. The third young man was by far the best musician of the three. Everyone agreed that the decision of the judges was wise and beyond dispute, but it helped the father of the girl not at all.

Days and weeks passed, and the three young men grew so anxious that they pitched their tents on the bank of the river near the girl's house. Daily their fathers pressed the girl's father for an answer so that their sons might return home and tend to their business and flocks again. But the girl's father simply could not make up his mind.

One day the girl was at the river washing clothes, and the young men were on the bank watching her. The girl slipped and fell into the river, and instantly a crocodile swam toward her.

The young musician seized his harp and played beautiful music. The music charmed the crocodile, and he stopped and rolled in the water with joy. Meanwhile, the marksman seized the rifle and shot the crocodile. And the strong young man jumped into the water and saved the girl before she was swept downstream.

They carried the girl to her house, and with the help of a wise doctor she regained the flush of life and began to breathe. As soon as she was awake, all three suitors began to argue.

"I should have her," the harpist said. "For I was first to act. If I had not charmed the beast, your efforts would have been wasted."

"False," cried the marksman. "Your music delayed the crocodile for only an instant. In that instant, I shot him. I should have her."

"Wrong, wrong, both of you," the strong young man insisted. "Even if she were saved from the crocodile, the river would have taken her. I saved her from the river. She should be mine."

The camel driver stopped talking and smiled at us. "Did you like that story?" he asked.

"But how did it end?" we asked.

"I don't know," the camel driver said. "In life there are no perfect endings; problems just go on and on. Perhaps that is what this story tells us."

"People don't like stories that have no endings," we said. "There must be an ending."

"Very well," the camel driver agreed. "Here is your ending. The case went before the three wise judges again. The first judge said that the girl should go to the harpist. The second judge said she should go to the marksman. The third judge said the girl should go to the strong swimmer. There is your ending."

"But it isn't an ending," we protested. "Nothing has been decided."

"Nothing is ever decided in this life," the camel driver answered. "But here is another ending for you. The father, in desperation, finally decided to leave the choice up to the girl. From that time on, women have been allowed to choose their husbands. That will make the story interesting—but false."

"And whom did she choose?" we asked.

The camel driver laughed. "She could not make up her mind," he said. "I like that ending. It has some truth in it."

"But it is not an ending," we protested. "We are right back where we started."

The camel driver rose. "Good," he said. "Then I must go. If you want an ending for that story, you must find it for yourselves."

He drew his cloak across his face and walked away. The wind swept through the marketplace and hurled dust against us. The camel driver moved into the crowd and was gone.

"We'll get the end of that story," we said. "Somewhere in this country we'll find it."

We heard many stories in our travels, but we did not find the ending to the one about the three suitors. And so we must tell you what the camel driver told us: If you want an ending for the story, you must find it for yourself.

# 16
# The Talkative Turtle

**B**esides the hyena man and the camel driver, we found only one other Somali storyteller, an old teacher. We told him that we had not met many Somalis who liked to talk. The old teacher smiled. "Perhaps it is the wind and sand," he said. "People like to keep their mouths closed."

After a moment he added, "There is a story that they tell out on the desert. The Danakil tell it, and the Somali tell it. The Danakil say it is their story, but it probably comes from somewhere else." And then he told us this story of the turtle who could not keep his mouth closed.

A turtle who lived in the Awash River had watched the birds fly and the fish swim and the antelope run. The turtle, who had spent his entire life creeping on the ground, wished to move as swiftly as the other creatures. Most of all he wished to move through the sky like the birds. He wished to go swiftly and fly high.

One day the turtle said to the eagles, "Take me into the sky with you so I can move swiftly and fly high."

"It can be done," the eagles said. "You have strong jaws. If you grasp a stick very hard and hold on tightly, we can fly with you in the sky. But you must never open your mouth."

The turtle agreed to this. The eagles took both ends of a stick, the turtle grasped the middle of the stick in his mouth, and the great birds soared into the sky. The turtle hung on tightly to the stick. He enjoyed flying swift and high through the sky.

The eagles flew over a village, and swooped low to look at some children playing in a field. The children looked up and saw the flying turtle. "Look at that silly turtle!" they cried. "Why is he not walking on the ground as turtles are supposed to?"

The eagles soared up again, but the turtle had heard the children. He shouted angrily at them. "I'm not a silly turtle. I can fly—."

When the turtle opened his mouth, he lost his hold on the stick and began to tumble toward the ground, all the while shouting, "I can fly-y-y-y—." He kept saying it until he hit the ground.

When the Somali teacher finished his story, we said, "The story makes clear that sometimes a person should keep his mouth shut. But we agree that the Danakil did not make up the story. We believe it was told first in India."

"The story tells a truth about life," the old Somali said. "And the truth travels far."

# Afterword

Have four decades really gone by since Russ Davis and I traveled the scary mountain roads of Ethiopia in our Land Rover and drove the long and lonely distances of the great Rift Valley? Sometimes it seems to me like four years ago or four months or even yesterday that we were there. But that is a trick memory plays when we think about people and events that were and still are important to us.

Yes, forty years have passed, and Ethiopia has changed dramatically since we were there. When Russ and I and our families arrived in Addis Ababa in 1955, Haile Selassie was the all-powerful emperor of Ethiopia. If any monarch in the world seemed secure, it was surely the Conquering Lion of Judah. At that time Ethiopia was tranquil within its own borders and relatively at peace with its neighbors. Rains and harvests were good, and food was plentiful.

How quickly that time of peace and plenty ended! In the 1960s and 1970s strong independence movements began in the provinces of Eritrea and Tigray; the Oromo people started a liberation front. Fighting broke out in several areas. In 1974, Emperor Haile Selassie was overthrown; the army assumed control of the country, and Ethiopia was declared a republic with a socialist form of government. In 1977, the neighboring country of Somalia attacked Ethiopia. The purpose of the invasion was to annex a part of Ethiopia called the Ogaden, where the population is mainly Somali people. The Somali army was thrown back, but at great cost in lives and money. Most terrible of all, devastating droughts enveloped largely agricultural Ethiopia in the 1970s and 1980s, and the resulting famines killed an estimated one million people.

Somehow the country has survived. Eritrea gained its independence in 1993, but otherwise Ethiopia has not broken apart or sunk into anarchy. It is struggling against great odds to confront its problems of hunger, disease, poverty, and political instability. Ethiopia will never again be the country that Russ and I knew. But the people we knew are the same, and they will be the backbone of the country as they have been since ancient times.

I am glad that we were in Ethiopia at the time we were. I am glad that we could have a hand, if only a small one, in helping to preserve the oral traditions of a very special part of Africa.

# Glossary

Ato (ah'-toe)    equivalent to the English "Mr."

Cherak (cheer'-äk)    a mythical, man-eating monster

Grazmatch (gräz'-mätch)    a military officer who commands the left flank in battle. Not used in the modern military.

Injera (in-jer'-uh)    a spongy, flat bread made of an indigenous Ethiopian grain called *t'eff* (akin to millet). Other grains such as wheat are sometimes used to make injera.

Kenyazmatch (ken-yäz'-mätch)    a military officer who commands the right flank in battle. No longer used in the modern Ethiopian army.

Ras (räs)    a high official, either civilian or military, in charge of a region or political subdivision of Ethiopia.

Shamma (sham'-mä)    a long shawl usually made of

loosely woven white cotton cloth. All *shammas* have
a border of bright colors. The *shamma* is worn by
both Ethiopian men and women.

TUKAL (too'-kul)          a rectangular, one-room dwelling
made of mud. Always built with a conical thatched
roof, the *tukal* is the traditional house of Ethiopian
villagers.

WAT (wät)          a hot, spicy pepper sauce which is made
into a stew with chicken, beef, or mutton and
sometimes, in the arid regions, with goat or camel
meat. *Wat* is probably Ethiopia's most popular
dish.

WOIZERO (woe'-zuh-roe)          equivalent to the English
"Mrs."